Who Pooped? in the Park

in the Park

written by Gary D. Robson · illustrations by Elijah Brady Clark

FARCOUNTRY
PRESS

To my wife, Kathy, who's had to step in a lot
of what this book's about since I dragged
her out here in the country with me.
Thanks for putting up with me.

ISBN 10: 1-56037-273-7
ISBN 13: 978-1-56037-273-8

© 2004 Farcountry Press
Text © 2004 Gary D. Robson

Who Pooped in the Park? is a registered trademark of Farcountry Press,
a division of Lee Enterprises.

For more information about our books, write Farcountry Press, P.O. Box 5630,
Helena, MT 59604; call (800) 821-3874; or visit www.farcountrypress.com.

Manufactured by:
Bolvo Yuanzhou Midas Printing Ltd.
Bolvo Yuanzhou Town Xianan Administration District
Huizhou, Guangdong
People's Republic of China
February 2011
Printed in China.

Created, produced, and designed in the United States.

15 14 13 12 11   8 9 10 11 12

"Dad? I have to go to the bathroom." Michael squirmed in the back seat.

"We'll be at our campground in just half an hour," said Dad.
"We're in Yellowstone National Park now."

"He's just nervous," said Michael's sister. "He thinks a bear's gonna eat him."
She growled at Michael and made her fingers look like claws.

"Stop it, Emily," said Mom. "Nobody is getting eaten by anything."

Michael was very excited about the trip, but Emily was right. He was nervous. He had just read a book about grizzly bears. He knew how big they could get. He also knew that a hungry grizzly bear would eat just about anything—maybe even a boy.

"I *am* kind of scared of bears," admitted Michael.

"Don't worry," Dad told him. "We'll show you how to count a bear's toes and never get close enough to be scared."

"Here's our campsite. Let's set up the tent. Then we can go for a walk and I'll show you what I mean," Dad said. Michael was awfully worried about grizzly bear toes, but tried not to show it.

"Let's hurry!" said Emily. "I want to see some animals!"

Once the tent was up, the whole family went for a hike. Emily started to complain before they even left the campground. "I haven't seen any animals yet. Maybe there aren't any here!"

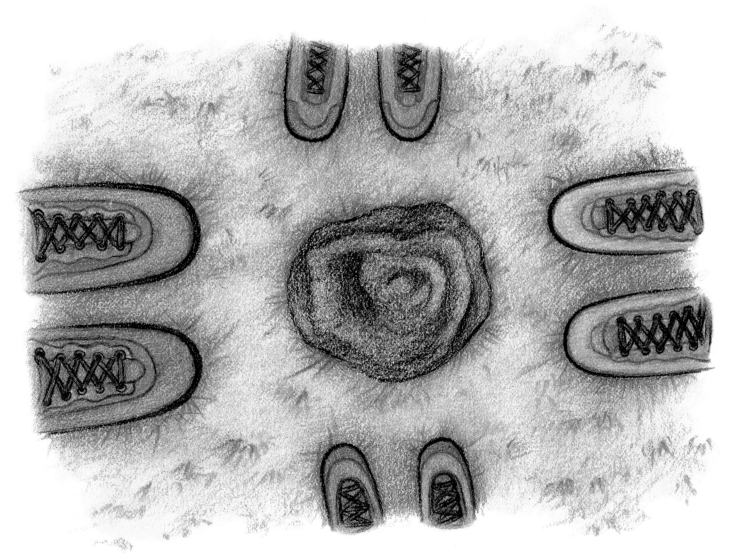

"There are definitely animals here," said Dad. "We're going to learn about them from their scat."

"Scat?" said Michael. "What's scat?"

"Scat is the word hikers and trackers use for animal poop," Mom said. "This big flat thing is bison poop. People call these buffalo chips."

"It looks hard," said Michael. "Not squishy like poop."

"Fresh bison poop *is* squishy," answered Dad. "But it dries out. You can tell how old it is by how hard it is."

American bison

water buffalo from India

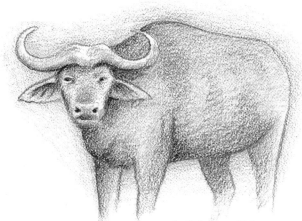

cape buffalo from Africa

"Bison?" said Emily. "I thought Mom said this was from a buffalo."

"Technically, they're called bison," Dad responded. "But early settlers called them buffalo because they look like buffaloes from other parts of the world, and the name stuck."

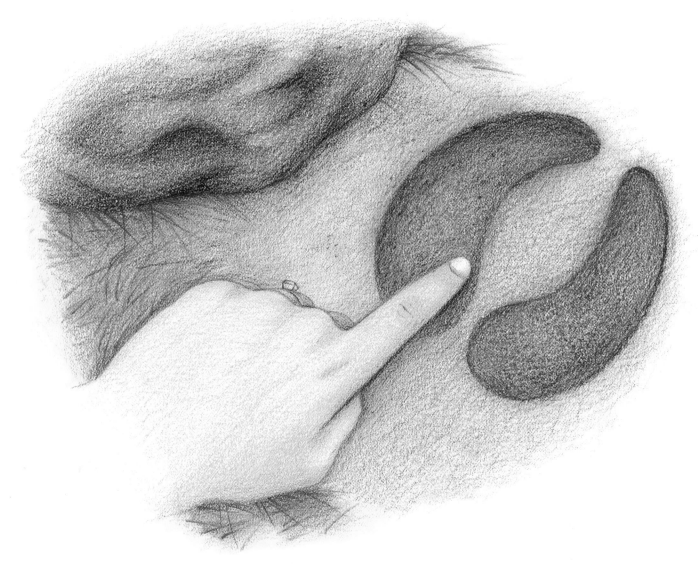

"Here are some bison tracks," said Mom.

"They have big feet," Emily giggled.

"Bison are the biggest animals in the Park," responded Dad. "Males weigh as much as a small car."

"That's bigger than a grizzly bear!" said Michael.

"See, Michael," said Dad. "We don't have to get up close to an animal to learn about it. Instead of a close encounter of the *scary* kind, we'll have a close encounter of the *poopy* kind."

Everybody laughed, and Mom made a gross-out face.

"Dad! Mom! Look over here! I found bunny scat!" yelled Michael. "It's just like what we have in Fluffy's cage."

"We came all the way to Yellowstone for *that?*" grumbled Emily. "Michael's bunny makes plenty of poop at home."

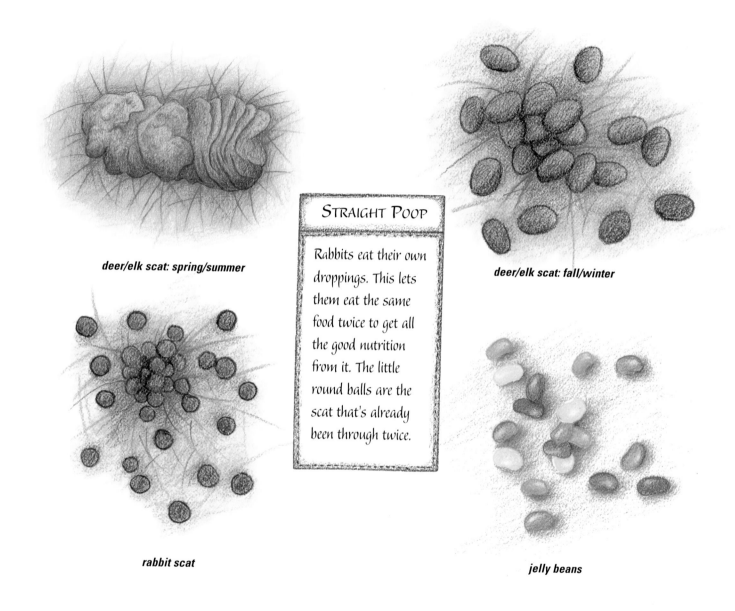

deer/elk scat: spring/summer

deer/elk scat: fall/winter

rabbit scat

jelly beans

"That's not from a rabbit," said Mom, "It's from a deer."

"Right! Bunny poop looks like little round balls," added Dad. "Deer scat is shaped more like jellybeans."

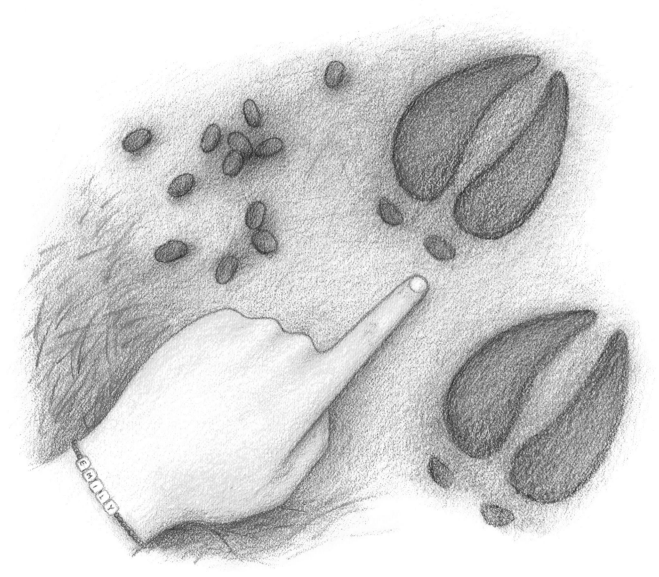

"Are these deer tracks?" Michael asked.

"Yes!" said Mom. "See how they're split? Like bison tracks, only smaller."

"Pointier, too," added Emily. She was starting to get interested. "But what are these marks?"

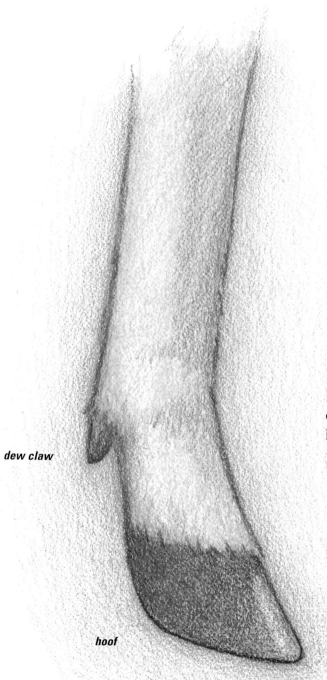

dew claw

hoof

"Those are from his dew claws," said Mom. "They're little claws behind the hoof. Dew claws sometimes show in deer tracks in soft ground, but not in bison tracks."

Female deer, elk, and moose don't grow antlers. Reindeer are the only members of the deer family where both males and females have antlers.

"Oh, no!" said Michael. "Here's one of his antlers. Did a bear eat him?" Michael looked around nervously.

"No, he's fine. Deer and elk shed their antlers every winter and then grow a new, bigger set the next year. This antler is from an elk."

"This elk was in a hurry, though," said Mom, as she studied the ground.

Michael and Emily went over to look.

"How can you tell?" said Michael.

stotting or pronking

galloping

walking

"The hoofprints get very far apart here," Mom explained, "and the back prints are in front of the front prints."

"He was walking backwards?" said Emily.

"No, he was galloping. Something scared him and he was moving fast."

"I know what scared him," Dad called.

The family hurried over to look.

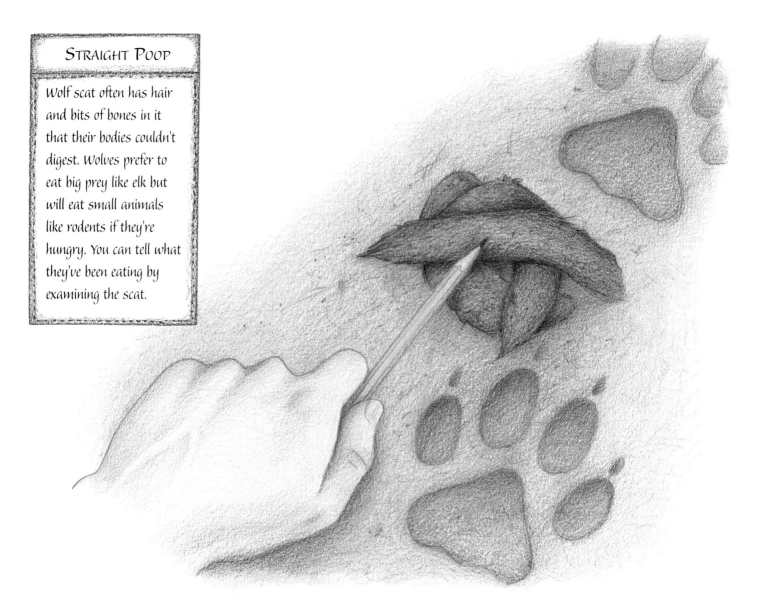

"This is wolf scat," Dad said, "and there are wolf tracks all around here."

"They look like dog tracks," said Michael.

"Big ones!" Emily added.

STRAIGHT POOP

All the wolves in Yellowstone were killed years ago, but gray wolves from Canada were reintroduced in 1995, and now Yellowstone has over 100 wolves.

"Most of the tracks are shallow," Mom pointed out, "but these are very deep and the dirt is pushed up behind them."

"That's where the wolf launched himself toward the elk and started chasing him," explained Dad.

"Did the wolf get him?" Michael asked.

"I don't think so," said Mom. "Look!"

Far across the meadow, they saw two wolves lying in the sun.

As they walked along the trail into the woods, Michael looked all over for tracks.

"Look, everyone! I found another wolf track."

wolf track

mountain lion track

"That's not a wolf track," said Dad. "It doesn't show any claw marks, and the front of the big pad looks dented in."

"You found a mountain lion track," said Mom.

"Let's look for mountain lion poop," said Michael.

"I don't think you'll find any," said Mom, "but you can look."

"Wow! There's a huge pile right here in the middle of the trail."

"That's not from a mountain lion. All you can see in it is vegetables and something that looks like oats," said Dad.

STRAIGHT POOP

Horses walk while they poop, but they stop and stand still to pee.

"It's horse poop!" said Emily.

"Right," said Mom. "People ride horses out here. See if you can find any tracks."

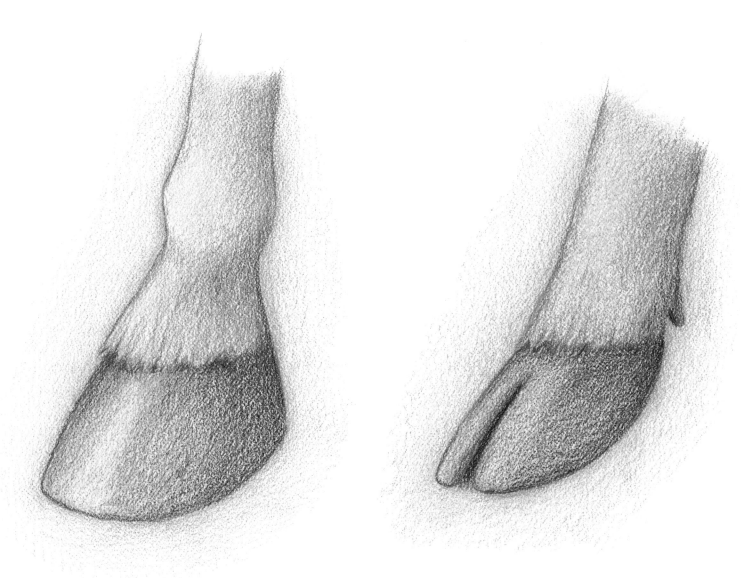

Michael found tracks, all right, but they didn't look like he expected.

"That's an awfully funny-shaped hoof," he said.

"Horses don't have split hooves like bison and deer," said Dad,
"It's just one part."

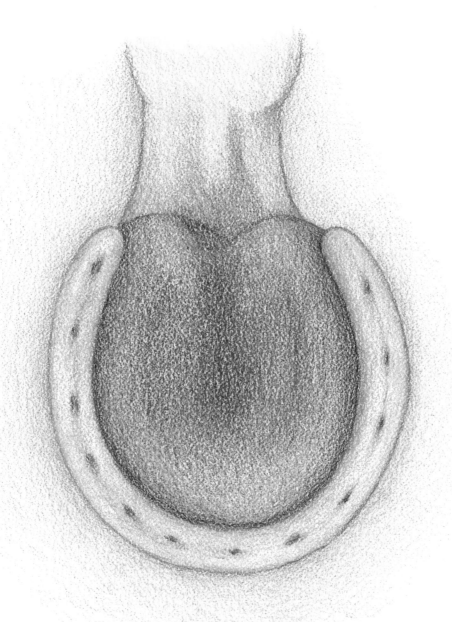

"He means the shoe," said Mom.

Michael looked puzzled and Dad laughed. "Horses that are ridden a lot have metal shoes to keep their hooves from wearing down. That's the track you're seeing."

"What are these tracks over here?" asked Emily. She was kneeling by a hole in the ground looking at some tracks.

Dad took a close look. "Check out those long claw marks, kids!"

"Is it from a bear?" Michael said with a shudder.

"No," said Dad. "These are badger tracks, and that's the hole he lives in."

"His claws are huge," said Emily.

"That's how he digs the holes," Mom answered. "He uses those front feet and claws like shovels and picks."

Michael followed the tracks backward from
the hole and spotted some big hoofprints.

"I found more bison prints over here!"

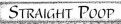
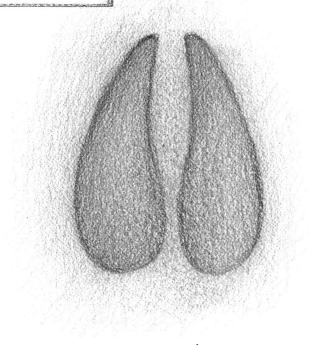

moose track

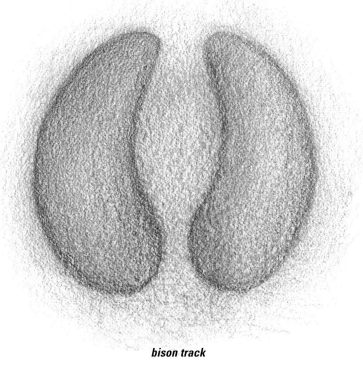

bison track

"Those aren't bison prints," Dad pointed out. "They're much pointier and not nearly as wide."

"Right," said Mom. "They're definitely moose tracks."

"Moose like to hang out near streams and lakes to eat water plants," said Dad, "but they come into the forests a lot, too."

"Whoa, Dad! What happened to this tree? Did the moose do that?"

"Something was sharpening its claws, Michael. And if you look how high those scratch marks go, it was pretty big!"

"It's not just the animal that's big," said Emily.
"Look at the size of this poop!"

"It looks like we found your grizzly bear," said Dad.
"Let's see what you learned today. What can you
figure out about this bear?"

"He's taller than you, and he has really long claws," said Michael.

"He's been eating plants," said Emily, "because there's no hair or bones in here."

"Good!" Mom said. "What else?"

STRAIGHT POOP

Grizzlies eat almost anything. They like fish and many kinds of plants, roots, and berries. Grizzlies can hunt their own meat, but they often steal kills away from wolves and other predators. They even eat moths and other insects.

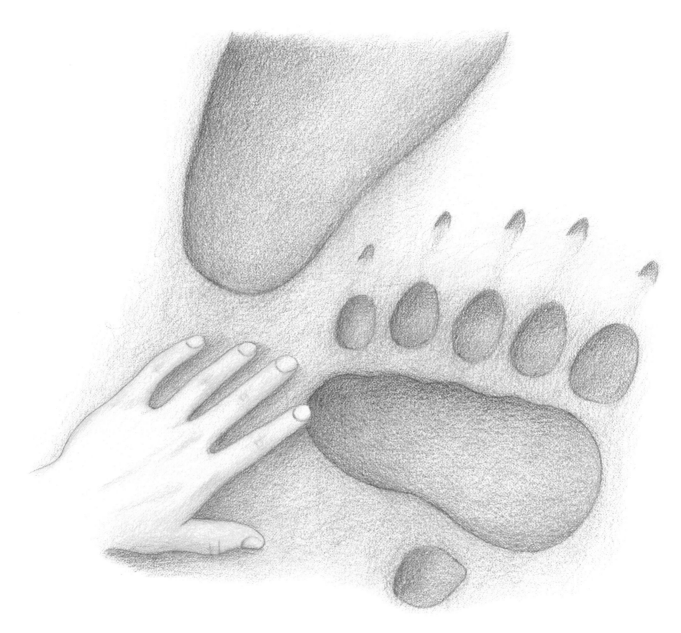

"Here's his footprint," said Michael. "It's huge! He has more toes than a wolf, and his claws are longer than my fingers."

"I told you you'd be able to count a grizzly's toes," laughed Dad.

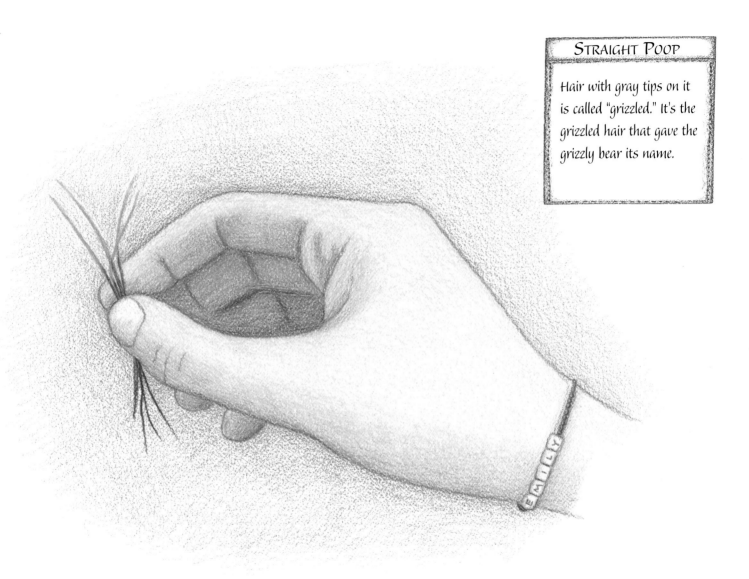

STRAIGHT POOP

Hair with gray tips on it is called "grizzled." It's the grizzled hair that gave the grizzly bear its name.

"He rubbed off some hair on the tree," said Emily. "It's really dark, but the tips are gray."

"Just like Dad's," smiled Mom.

"Don't pick on me," Dad grinned back.

As they ate dinner that night, everyone talked about how much fun they had.

"We didn't see very many animals," said Emily, "but it seemed like we did."

"And I didn't get scared once," said Michael.

Tracks and Scat Notes

Grizzly Bear
Very big tracks show large claw marks. Scat changes depending on diet. Claw marks show high on trees.

Rabbit
Small tracks filled in between toes. Scat is little balls.

Mule Deer
Pointy split-hoof tracks. Scat is long and oval-shaped like jellybeans, not round like a rabbit's.

Elk
Tracks are longer and more blunt than that of a deer. Scat is quite a bit bigger than that of deer.

Horse
Tracks are almost as big as that of a bison or elk, but wider and not split. Scat is in chunks, with roughage from vegetation often visible.

Moose
Tracks are bigger than that of an elk and much pointier. Scat is a lot like that of elk.

Bison
Tracks are as long as moose tracks but much wider and blunt tipped. Scat looks like cow patties.

Gray Wolf
Tracks are like a dog's, as big as a kid's hand. Claw marks usually show. Scat is very dark colored with tapered ends.

Mountain Lion
Tracks are almost as big as a wolf's, but claws don't show. Scat is rarely seen because they bury it.

Badger
Tracks show very long front claws connected to the toes. Scat is rarely seen.

The Author

Gary Robson owns a bookstore in Red Lodge, Montana, and lives on a ranch near Yellowstone National Park. He has written about a wide variety of subjects for both children and adults and taught at several colleges in Montana and California. He is an expert on closed captioning technology for deaf and hard-of-hearing people. Visit www.whopooped.com for more information on Gary's books.

The Illustrator

Elijah Brady Clark lives in Bozeman, Montana, where he graduated from Montana State University with a degree in fine arts and graphic design. He works as an illustrator and designer. He grew up in the Flathead Valley near Glacier National Park and moved to Bozeman in 1999. He spends most of his time enjoying his two favorite passions, art and the outdoors.

BOOKS IN THE
WHO POOPED IN THE PARK?
SERIES:

Acadia National Park

Big Bend National Park

Black Hills

Colorado Plateau

Death Valley National Park

Glacier National Park

Grand Canyon National Park

Grand Teton National Park

Great Smoky Mountains National Park

Northwoods

Olympic National Park

Red Rock Canyon National Conservation Area

Rocky Mountain National Park

Sequoia and Kings Canyon National Parks

Shenandoah National Park

Sonoran Desert

Yellowstone National Park

Yosemite National Park